The Emigrant Indians of Kansas

BIBLIOGRAPHICAL SERIES
*The Newberry Library Center
for the History of the American Indian*

General Editor
Francis Jennings

Assistant Editor
William R. Swagerty

The Center is Supported by Grants from

The National Endowment for the Humanities
The Ford Foundation
The W. Clement and Jessie V. Stone Foundation
The Woods Charitable Fund, Inc.
Mr. Gaylord Donnelley

The Emigrant Indians of Kansas

A Critical Bibliography

WILLIAM E. UNRAU

Published for the Newberry Library

Indiana University Press

BLOOMINGTON AND LONDON

Manufactured in the United States of America

Library of Congress Cataloging in Publication Data

Unrau, William E   1929–
    The emigrant Indians of Kansas.

    (The Newberry Library Center for the History of the American Indian bibliographical series)
    Includes index.
    1. Indians of North America—Kansas—Bibliography. 2. Indians of North America—Kansas—Government relations—Bibliography. I. Title. II. Series: Bibliographical series.
Z1209.2.U52K358 [E78.K16]   016.9781'004'97   79–2169
ISBN 0–253–36816–2 pbk. 1 2 3 4 5 83 82 81 80 79

CONTENTS

INTRODUCTION

From the English invasion of Virginia in the early seventeenth century to the closing years of the nineteenth century, the forced displacement of native American people has been a tragically recurring theme in North American history. Land hunger, fanatic quests for furs and precious metals, the struggle for imperial advantage, misguided assumptions regarding cultural superiority, and the deployment of a more sophisticated military technology prompted the nation-states of western Europe to dispossess Indian peoples almost at will.

After the War of Independence the United States lost little time in refining the strategy of Indian displacement. At the same time the young nation devoted much attention to constructing a moral and legal justification for its acquisitive actions. Outright military campaigns, like the Battle of Fallen Timbers (1794), the Black Hawk War (1832), and the Seminole War (1835), were less susceptible to righteous justification than were the more subtle techniques of treaty-making, disruption of tribal leadership, and government failure to honor the promises and responsibilities of forced wardship. Yet the ultimate results were no less devastating than the application of powder and lead—certainly not for the more than ten thousand native Americans who were forced to emigrate from the Old Northwest to the future Kansas in the decade and a half after 1830.

Because these forced migrations involved the movement of more than a dozen tribes and factions of tribes to a crazy-quilt pattern of reservations in the eastern third of the present Kansas, the serious student of Indian emigration should regularly consult two basic reference works. They are Charles J. Kappler's five-volume *Indian Affairs: Laws and Treaties* [96], of which volume 2 provides verbatim copies of all official federal Indian treaties; and Charles C. Royce's *Indian Land Cessions in the United States* [151], which provides detailed maps and statutory authority for all the reservations in the United States.

Since the majority of the documents regarding Indian culture, specific tribes, or topics relating to Indian affairs and migrations were recorded by White people, a biased, distorted, or even falsified perspective is often present. In the case of the Kansas emigrants, however, influential and well-educated mixed-bloods exerted considerable influence in tribal matters. These individuals wrote letters to government officials and magazines; they made speeches that were reproduced in newspapers, and their testimony was occasionally recorded in official government documents. While often biased themselves, these records are a valuable source for the historian, particularly if they are placed in a comparative, critical framework. A good example of such material is an article on the Potawatomi leader Wah-bahn-se, which was written by the Potawatomi mixed-blood and business council member J. N. Bourassa. It first appeared in a Kansas City newspaper in 1857 and more recently has been reprinted in the *Kansas Historical Quarterly* [24].

Two general interpretive works are crucial to an understanding of the dilemma faced by the emigrant Indians of Kansas in the 1830s and 1840s. In his *Seeds of Extinction: Jeffersonian Philanthropy and the American Indian* [156], Bernard W. Sheehan describes how government philanthropy in the form of an evolving removal policy was in fact more detrimental to Indian survival than the antagonistic behavior of the White frontier population. This distortion and eventual demise of Enlightenment ideals and environmental theory, says Sheehan, provide the most reasonable explanation of this apparent paradox. How a democratically oriented America committed to humanitarianism prevented the total destruction of native American life, while at the same time allowing its intractable code of economic individualism to erode the very resources needed to prevent Indian suffering, is the subject of Robert F. Berkhofer, Jr.'s, *The White Man's Indian: Images of the American Indian from Columbus to the Present* [18]. In a profound statement wholly applicable to the Kansas tribes, Berkhofer concludes that Indian people eventually became persuaded of their own inferiority and cooperated in their own ethnic destruction.

No less significant for a general understanding of the cultural and historical framework of the Kansas tribes in the early national period are Lucy Wales Kluckhohn's revision of Clark Wissler, *Indians of the United States* [183], and Wilcomb E. Washburn's *The*

Indian in America [178]. While sometimes criticized for being too sympathetic to the native American point of view, Washburn displays a firm command of his subject matter and is especially informative for the colonial period and first half of the nineteenth century. No earnest student of Indian ethnohistory can afford to ignore his sensitive treatment of attempted cultural destruction.

RECOMMENDED WORKS

For the Beginner

[58]   Grant Foreman, *The Last Trek of the Indians.*
[125]   H. Craig Miner and William E. Unrau, *The End of Indian Kansas: A Study of Cultural Revolution, 1854–1871.*
[155]   George A. Schultz, *An Indian Canaan: Isaac McCoy and the Vision of an Indian State.*
[178]   Wilcomb E. Washburn, *The Indian in America.*
[183]   Clark Wissler, *Indians of the United States.*

Additional Titles For a Basic Library Collection

[7]   Bert Anson, *The Miami Indians.*
[16]   Robert F. Berkhofer, Jr., *Salvation and the Savage: An Analysis of Protestant Missions and American Indian Response, 1787–1862.*
[27]   Martha B. Caldwell, ed., *Annals of the Shawnee Methodist Mission and Indian Manual Training School.*
[38]   James A. Clifton, *The Prairie People: Continuity and Change in Potawatomi Indian Culture, 1665–1965.*
[59]   Otto F. Frederikson, *The Liquor Question among the Indian Tribes in Kansas, 1804–1881.*

BIBLIOGRAPHICAL ESSAY

Historical Setting and Cultural Identification

During the second quarter of the nineteenth century much of the land lying between the Ohio River and the Great Lakes was still retained by native Americans. But White land hunger and the federal government's Indian removal policy soon altered the situation drastically. By midcentury nearly all of the resident Algonkian and Iroquoian people had been forced to cede their reservations in the Old Northwest and take up residence in a distant place called Kansas.

To accomplish this momentous displacement the White invaders utilized a variety of devices—some legal, some quasi-legal, and some wholly illegal—and with unwavering ethnocentrism rationalized their actions in the name of Christian civilization and natural progress. In less than two decades, by the mid-1870s, these very same emigrant tribes had been expelled from Kansas, with only a few of the more traditionalist factions remaining behind to be further exploited by the new horde of White farmers, land jobbers, and corporate interests who rushed into Kansas after passage of the Kansas-Nebraska Bill of 1854. Collectively, these displacements constitute one of the great tragedies in modern Indian-White relations, and the published literature on this disaster is worthy of critical appraisal.

As fifteen states were added to the United States during the first half of the nineteenth century, its population grew by nearly 18,000,000—from 5,297,000 in 1800 to 23,261,000 in 1850. This remarkable increment was especially evident in the new states of Ohio, Indiana, Illinois, Michigan, and Wisconsin, whose collective native American population was forced to cede land and make room for White farmers, merchants, and industrial workers. Beverly W. Bond, Jr., *The Civilization of the Old Northwest* [23], and R. Carlyle Buley, *The Old Northwest: Pioneer Period, 1815–1840* [26], provide informative but excessively simplified overviews of this White invasion, while in *The First and Second United States Empires: Governors and Territorial Government, 1784–1912* [50] Jack E. Eblen points more directly to the imperial strategy that guided United States expansion into the lower Great Lakes country and the Mississippi and Ohio valleys. A victory over the British, says Eblen, was supposed to improve the lot of the Indians, but the real consequences were increased native resentment and the refinement of moral arguments for future White expansion. The devastating impact of the War of 1812 on the Indians of this region is carefully analyzed in Reginald Horsman, *Expansion and American Indian Policy, 1783–1812* [87].

In terms of numbers and the strength they displayed in the struggle against emigration, the major tribes were the Delawares, Kickapoos, Miamis, Ottawas, Potawatomis, Sacs and Foxes, and Shawnees. All were members of the Algonkian cultural-linguistic family and had experienced varying degrees of dispossession and acculturation before their removal to the area west of

Missouri. The minor tribes (or factions of tribes) were the Algonkian Chippewas, Kaskaskias, Peorias, Piankashaws, and Weas; Munsee and Stockbridge bands; and, farther west, the Siouan Iowas, Kansas, Osages, Otoes, Missouris, and Quapaws. The Wyandots, a remnant band of the former Huron Confederacy, and the powerful Cherokees were marginally involved in the struggle to maintain their culture and land titles in the future Kansas. Ethnohistorical summaries of all of these tribes can be found in *The Handbook of American Indians North of Mexico* [80], edited by Frederick W. Hodge. Since a substantial body of research on Indian affairs has been published since the two Hodge volumes were released more than sixty years ago, a new and expanded edition is currently being prepared under the general editorship of William C. Sturtevant [81]. Additional information of a general nature is available in *Report with Respect to the House Resolution Authorizing the Committee on Interior and Insular Affairs to Conduct an Investigation of the Bureau of Indian Affairs* [142], released by the United States government in 1953. The major portion of this book is an alphabetical listing of the major tribes and a brief discussion of the treaties, laws, and material events that have affected the individual tribes up to 1952.

Old but still useful for an understanding of Indian culture in the Old Northwest before removal is Emma Helen Blair, ed., *The Indian Tribes of the Upper Mississippi Valley and Region of the Great Lakes* [21], which presents the observations of White traders and travelers such as Bacqueville de la Potherie and Nicholas Perrot. A young native American scholar, R. David Edmunds, has recently published *The Potawatomis: Keepers of the Fire* [54], a well-documented study of the forced acculturation dating back to the early seventeenth century that finally led to the tragic removals of the Potawatomi people during the Jacksonian era. In his *Social Organization of the Central Algonkian Indians* [28], Charles Callender describes how the impact of the American Revolution forced a shift of the fur trade from upper Great Lakes to the Old Northwest. White farmers made hunting less effective, and while the basic framework of exchange continued, the native economy came to be dominated by annuity monies derived from the repeated sale of land. The worst aspect of the emerging system was that the new income came to be controlled by White merchants working in league with government officials and self-made "chiefs." As the hereditary chiefs lost their influence and old sanctions diminished in importance, social and political disorganization were the outcome. This situation was aggravated in the period following the War of 1812, when the federal government sought and secured allegiance treaties with the Sacs and Foxes, the Potawatomis, the Kickapoos, and other Algonkian peoples, as Robert L. Fisher has demonstrated in the "The Treaties of Portage des Sioux" [56].

Taking a close look at the situation in one state, Leon M. Gordon, II, "The Red Man's Retreat from Northern Indiana" [70], describes in great detail how the Potawatomis, Miamis, and Weas were routinely victimized by such traders as George W. and William G.

Ewing and Lathrop M. Taylor. The consequent inflation of market prices for flour and bacon was so great that complaints were voiced not only by the Indian rank and file, but by the White settlers as well. With credit to individual Indian leaders running as high as $3,000 and undersized blankets selling for as much as $25, the traders were as determined to keep the Indians under their control as the White settlers were anxious to have them removed. That too much emphasis on warfare and scalp-taking for pay by Whites has clouded the fact that the majority of land cessions arranged in this period were overreaching and basically unfair is the conclusion of Walter H. Blumenthal, *American Indians Dispossessed: Fraud in Land Cessions Forced upon the Tribes* [22].

In a controversial but suggestive study titled *Keepers of the Game: Indian-Animal Relationships and the Fur Trade* [116], Calvin Martin attempts to challenge the belief that the eastern Algonkians (specifically the Micmacs and Ojibwas, who had some contact with the Ohio and Great Lakes tribes) practiced a relationship of mutual courtesy with their wildlife brethren. As hunting became a more secular enterprise, says Martin, the eastern Algonkians became as exploitative as their White detractors, thus destroying much of the game that might otherwise have made them less vulnerable to removal.

Martin's analysis, which has not gone unchallenged, is one illustration of new approaches to the writing of Indian history and anthropology. In his "Political Context of a New Indian History" [17], Robert F. Berkhofer, Jr., chastises historians for focusing too much on

Indian-White relations and anthropologists for naively advocating the Indian point of view based on uncritical oral accounts and misguided notions regarding the nature of cultural persistence. More particularly applied to those Indians who were forced to move to distant Kansas, Berkhofer's complaint that erring historians have confused an Indian culture with an Indian political tribe is an important consideration. The fact is, as Berkhofer emphasizes, political authority among Indian people before White contact was territorially and functionally much smaller than those groups later designated "tribal" by agencies of the federal government or the typical White settler. Certainly by the time the various Indian groups arrived in Kansas they were rent asunder by factionalism and sociopolitical squabbles that were virtually irreversible. The emerging ideology of Manifest Destiny during the second quarter of the nineteenth century played a no less important role in distorting the public perception of what was really happening to the Indians. Caught up in the ethnocentric assertions of White expansionists, American science endorsed the popular belief that the Indians were simply not worth saving. This is the argument depicted by Reginald Horsman in his "Scientific Racism and the American Indian in the Mid-nineteenth Century" [89]. American science not only dismissed philanthropists as misguided optimists, but articulated irrational fears regarding the genetic mixing of Indians and Mexicans as well. Given these views and circumstances, all that was needed for a massive exodus of Indians from the Old Northwest was a basic alteration in federal Indian policy.

Changing Federal Indian Policy

Proposals for an Indian state far removed from the negative influences of White land jobbers go back to the very beginnings of the American nation. Because many of these seemingly positive remedies had a direct bearing on the future of the Ohio valley and lower Lakes tribes, the literature on Indian removal in the early national period is especially important to an understanding of the later migration to Kansas.

The intellectual foundation of removal, with all its contradictions and paradoxes, has been carefully analyzed by Bernard W. Sheehan in his *Seeds of Extinction: Jeffersonian Philanthropy and the American Indian* [156]. Two old but still valuable studies of Indian removal in the infant and adolescent stages have been published by Annie Heloise Abel. They are "The History of Events Resulting in Indian Consolidation West of the Mississippi" [1], and "Proposals for an Indian State, 1778–1878" [2], both published by the American Historical Association shortly after the turn of the century. Abel was one of the first scholars to make extensive use of the voluminous Indian Office manuscript collections in the National Archives, and her scholarship had a profound effect on the work of James C. Malin. Whereas Abel directed her attention more to the southern tribes who eventually were removed to the future eastern Oklahoma, Malin examined the situation as it developed in future Kansas. In his *Indian Policy and Westward Expansion* [111], Malin pointed to the contrived enculturation scheme underlying the government's removal plan. Emphasizing the role played by Indian Commissioner William Medill in the development of the two-reservation system as a means of opening the central corridor for transcontinental railroad construction, Malin concluded that technology and government duplicity sealed the fate of the emigrant tribes. For additional background to removal, the student should consult Reginald Horsman, *The Origins of Indian Removal, 1815–1824* [88], and Francis Paul Prucha, "The Image of the Indian in Pre–Civil War America" [140]. Prucha contends that President Jefferson perceived no essential contradiction between civilizing the Indian and taking his land base east of the Mississippi River. War Secretary Lewis Cass, President Andrew Jackson, and even Horace Greeley were generally optimistic regarding the removal program as an instrument for improving Indian life through education, agriculture, the Christian churches, and isolation from the anticivilizing influences of White frontiersmen. Only Francis Parkman, says Prucha, held little hope for the removed Indian's survival. Dale Van Every's engagingly written *Disinherited: The Lost Birthright of the American Indian* [173] is biased in favor of the Indians and, like so many other works chronicling the events leading to removal, virtually ignores the northern removals in favor of an extensive discussion of the Cherokee tragedy in the South. In fact, with the exception of Donald J. Berthrong's "John Beach and the Removal of the Sauk and Fox from Iowa" [19] and James A. Clifton's *The Prairie*

People: Continuity and Change in Potawatomi Indian Culture, 1665–1965 [38], there is a paucity of substantial analyses of northern removals to compare with Mary E. Young's "The Creek Frauds: A Study in Conscience and Corruption" [185], her "Indian Removal and Land Allotment: The Civilized Tribes and Jacksonian Justice" [186], and Arthur H. DeRosier, Jr., *The Removal of the Choctaw Indians* [47].

The standard work on Indian removal and accompanying government legislation is Francis Paul Prucha, *American Indian Policy in the Formative Years: The Indian Trade and Intercourse Acts, 1790–1834* [135], which is complemented in somewhat oversimplified manner by George Dewey Harmon's older *Sixty Years of Indian Affairs, Political, Economic, and Diplomatic, 1789–1850* [82]. Harmon provided a reasonably systematic overview of the problem, but his discussion of the various removal treaties suffers from a failure to utilize many important Indian Office records and much correspondence on file in the National Archives.

Two significant studies of the land question, contemporary with the implementation of formal removal legislation during the first Jackson administration, are Robert W. McCluggage, "The Senate and Indian Land Titles, 1800–1825" [105], and Malcolm Rohrbough, *The Land Office Business: The Settlement and Administration of American Public Lands, 1789–1837* [148]. McCluggage contends that the breach between the executive and congressional departments over Indian policy formulation and administration encouraged the Senate to approve certain fee-simple Indian land allotments that under more amicable conditions would never have been approved. Because many of the allotments to tribal dignitaries were essential to the negotiation of land cession treaties by the emigrant Indians, bureaucratic obstruction at the highest levels contributed to social disorganization even before the long trek to Kansas. Rohrbough, on the other hand, describes the pressure brought to bear by White land jobbers operating in the region between the Appalachians and the Mississippi River during the period from the Land Ordinance of 1785 down to the Panic of 1837. Owing mainly to White disregard for Indian land titles in the Northwest and the continuing pressure of the speculators, conditions at the various frontier land offices deteriorated to the point of chaos.

Congressional passage of the Civilization Act of 1819 (which authorized a $10,000 annual appropriation) provided a financial vehicle for Christian missionary groups to become involved in the plan to acculturate the emigrant Indians once they had made the long trek to Kansas. Thomas McKenney, the first superintendent of the newly created Bureau of Indian Affairs in 1824, played an extremely important administrative role in the developing "civilization" program.

How McKenney attempted to mobilize public opinion in attracting ministerial support for removal is the thesis of Francis Paul Prucha, "Thomas L. McKenney and the New York Indian Board" [136]. In another article titled "American Indian Policy in the 1840s: Visions of Reform" [139], Prucha extols the positive role of missionaries who had their noblest efforts undermined almost beyond repair by the government's failure to enforce laws banning alcohol and White squatters from the Indian country as defined by the legislation of 1834. Precisely why the War Department failed to enforce the law, as in the case of the Delaware–Fort Leavenworth land speculation, is not at all clear, nor does Prucha deal with the widespread missionary appetite for land speculation in frontier Kansas. Herman J. Viola, in an extremely well documented biography of McKenney, *Thomas L. McKenney: Architect of America's Early Indian Policy, 1816–1830* [174], explains the Indian superintendent's firm commitment to removal policy and especially his close cooperation with the various missionary groups.

No one individual played a greater role in spotting out the promised land for the Old Northwest tribes than the Baptist missionary, government surveyor, and confidant of President Andrew Jackson, Isaac McCoy. In his *History of Baptist Indian Missions: Embracing Remarks on the Former and Present Condition of the Aboriginal Tribes; Their Settlement within the Indian Territory, and Their Future Prospects* [108], McCoy makes a plea for an Indian state, discusses various interdenominational problems, and presents some valuable ethnographic information regarding the tribes then residing in the future Kansas. Lela Barnes has edited the McCoy exploration journals of 1828 and 1830, in "Journal of Isaac McCoy for the Exploring Expedition of 1828" [106] and "Journal of Isaac McCoy for the Exploring Expedition of 1830" [107]. On these two occasions McCoy conducted certain

Potawatomi and Ottawa leaders to the Osage, Neosho, and lower Kaw valleys in Kansas. They visited the "savage" Kansas and Osages, as well as the reservation of the Shawnees near the mouth of the Kaw River. McCoy made a special point of advising government officials that the emigrant leaders were well aware of the more strategic and valuable reservation locations near the confluence of the Kaw and Missouri rivers. McCoy's son John, who later became preoccupied with land speculation in the vicinity of the future Kansas City, surveyed the reservation for a mixed band of Shawnees and New York Senecas, the reservations for the Ottawas, Peorias, Kaskaskias, Weas, Piankashaws, Kickapoos, and various parts of the future reservations for the Kansas, New York Iroquois, Wyandots, Sacs and Foxes, and Iowas. In an article published fifty years later, titled "Survey of Kansas Indian Lands" [109], the younger McCoy recalled with some regret the failure of a central seat of government for all the emigrant Indians of Kansas, whose lands he had surveyed in 1831. One of the better biographies of individuals closely involved in the removal of Indians from the lower Lakes country and the Ohio valley, George A. Schultz, *An Indian Canaan: Isaac McCoy and the Vision of an Indian State* [155], characterizes the elder McCoy as a truly visionary reformer. While he remained committed to Baptist orthodoxy, McCoy nevertheless was very critical of missionary groups who fought seemingly endless battles over the control of the several emigrant tribes. Schultz also points out that McCoy was interested in Indian languages and cultures in a scientific sense, that his desire for tribal improvement was remarkably sincere, and that his influence with high government officials was great. See also Emory J. Lyons, *Isaac McCoy: His Plan of and Work for Indian Colonization* [104].

While voluntary migration of a few Indians to the future Kansas — some bands of Shawnees, for example—-took place in the mid-1820s, it was not until passage of the first major removal bill in 1830 that the widespread movements of Indian peoples from the Old Northwest took place. Because of the human suffering involved and because the legislation was passed during the first administration of President Andrew Jackson—an alleged frontier type who, according to tradition, believed that military force was the only real solution to recalcitrant Indians—the orthodox interpretation has been to style Old Hickory as an Indian-hating chief executive with little sympathy for the well-being of the native American peoples east of the Mississippi. This conclusion, which has its roots in the Turnerian interpretation of the frontier experience and which continues to surface in the popular press and even in some modern survey textbooks, is indicative of the simplistic analysis of Indian affairs in the early national period.

In a psychoanalytic treatment of Jackson's alleged motives for removal, Michael Paul Rogin's *Fathers and Children: Andrew Jackson and the Subjugation of the American Indian* [147] asserts that for psychological reasons Old Hickory infantilized native Americans to such a degree that the onus of removal fell squarely on their own shoulders, although Rogin blames Jackson strongly. A more favorable, and certainly more scholarly, analysis of Jackson's Indian policy is Francis Paul Prucha's "Andrew Jackson's Indian Policy: A Reassessment" [138]. Emphasizing Jackson's firm interest in Indian welfare, Prucha insists that what appeared to be a distinctive anti-Indian sentiment was in fact mainly anti-British. Removal was the only sensible option for Indian survival. Prucha's revisionism, suggestive as it is, has not gone unchallenged. In two important articles, "Indian Removal Policy: Administrative, Historical and Moral Criteria for Judging Its Success or Failure" [176] and "Philanthropy and the American Indian: The Need for a Model" [177], Wilcomb E. Washburn takes issue with Prucha for downplaying the moral issues involved — for example, saving the native American people from ultimate extinction. A scholarly summary of Old Hickory's Indian policy that places strong emphasis on the problems facing the Indians in the Old Northwest is Ronald N. Satz, *American Indian Policy in the Jacksonian Era* [153]. Satz concludes that the Jacksonians refused to confront the basic constitutional problems of Indian nationality and took the easier path of enculturation as opposed to assimilation. Refusing to commit themselves to more responsibilities than were absolutely necessary, the Jacksonians were fearful of alienating the White public majority. They were caught up in nagging sectional tensions and territorial expansion, and they allowed self-seeking bureaucrats to exercise too much power. In the final analysis, says Satz, Jackson and his retinue wanted to remove Indians without undermining the foundations of their own political power. The complexity of the diverse issues involved is conveniently summarized in Francis Paul Prucha, *United States Indian Policy: A Critical Bibliography* [141].

The failure of France and Spain to colonize the Great Plains effectively is well analyzed in Henri Folmer, *Franco-Spanish Rivalry in North America, 1524–1763* [57]. From a documentary point of view Folmer's work should be augmented by A. P. Nasatir, ed., *Before Lewis and Clark: Documents Illustrating the History of Missouri, 1785–1804* [129], and Louise Barry's remarkably comprehensive annals of future Kansas, *The Beginning of the West* [13]. All these works underscore the fact that any major relocation of eastern Indians to the area west of Missouri was bound to create problems with whiskey merchants of the border region, the Osages, Kansas, Otoes, Pawnees, and the better mounted and armed tribes of the Great Plains. The unusual diversity of Indian culture in the future Kansas is expertly narrated in John Rydjord, *Indian Place-Names: Their Origin, Evolution, and Meanings, Collected in Kansas from the Siouan, Algonquian, Shoshonean, Caddoan, Iroquoian, and Other Tongues* [152].

Removal to the Kansas "Desert"

Largely owing to biased or oversimplified observations of such explorers as Lieutenant Zebulon M. Pike, Major Stephen H. Long, Dr. Edwin James, and Jacob

Fowler in the first two decades after the Louisiana Purchase, much of the future Kansas was designated "the Great American Desert." As a consequence government officials viewed the areas as a logical place to relocate Indians who needed to be isolated from the more corrupt representatives of White civilization and as a buffer zone against the hostile Plains Indians. That the Indians might serve as a barrier against British and Mexican advances from the west was also an important consideration. A general account of the desert controversy is W. Eugene Hollon, *The Great American Desert: Then and Now* [86], but more to the point with regard to the future of the Ohio and Indiana tribes is Francis Paul Prucha, "Indian Removal and the Great American Desert" [137]. Pointing out that the idea of removal dated back to the earliest years of the nineteenth century, Prucha emphasizes that the Indians of the Old Northwest were given ample time to select what they considered the most desirable lands immediately west of Missouri—lands that were anything but arid as defined by Pike, Long, and James. An excellent example of Indian visitation to the promised land is that of two educated mixed-blood Wyandots in 1831. Escorted to the area near the future site of Kansas City by government agent James B. Gardiner, Wyandot dignitaries William Walker and Silas Armstrong were favorably impressed with the topography and climate of the area. Their abrupt change of mind, however, was not because they were concerned that the "pagan" faction of their tribe might present an obstacle to their own designs for land speculation in that strategic area. The details of this conflict are well documented in J. Orin Oliphant's edition of "The Report of the Wyandot Exploring Delegation, 1831" [134].

A critical problem facing the government in its design to pave the way for removal was the extinguishing of historical, proprietary claims to the land from which the various emigrant reserves were to be carved. This is the theme of William E. Unrau's "United States 'Diplomacy' with the Dhegiha-Siouan Kansa, 1815–1825" [168]. By the treaty of 1825, the Kansa leadership agreed to relinquish its legal claim to the lower Kaw River valley between the present Topeka and Kansas City. Osage claims to the south and east were also extinguished, and in a supplementary Kansa treaty, engineered that same year in dubious circumstances, free and unmolested passage of Santa Fe Trail traders through the very heart of the now-diminished Kansa reservations was secured. The government insisted that both tribes adapt more rapidly to a sedentary, agricultural economy. Not surprisingly, as Bert Anson has demonstrated in his "Variations of the Indian Conflict: The Effect of the Emigrant Indian Removal Policy, 1830–1854" [6], the emigrant tribes were active agents in transmitting the more degrading customs of White culture to those Indians who had inhabited the Plains for at least two centuries, while in the meantime the emigrant people displayed a clear preference for the life of the hunt as opposed to the style of the sedentary horticulturist. In Anson's view, the least-explored aspect of emigrant policy is the negative influence of the partially acculturated Indian emigrants of the East upon their more isolated brethren in the West.

Long considered the standard study of Indian removal to Kansas (and eventually to the future Oklahoma) is Grant Foreman's *The Last Trek of the Indians* [58]. Foreman was an extremely prolific writer, and his talent for organizing vast amounts of data has seldom been matched. Recent research, however, involving studies of individual tribes that Foreman treated very generally, suggests that he was too preoccupied with the notion that the Indians of the Old Northwest were mostly helpless creatures who dutifully awaited the inevitable time when they would be herded together for the long and bloody march to inhospitable Kansas. In a journalistic fashion and relying heavily on Foreman's research, Gloria Jahoda has more recently attempted to breathe new life into the force and docility thesis in her *The Trail of Tears* [91]. The most sophisticated and comprehensive challenge to the Foreman-Jahoda interpretation is James A. Clifton's *The Prairie People: Continuity and Change in Potawatomi Indian Culture, 1665–1965* [38] and his "Chicago Was Theirs" [37]. Clifton argues that the more traditional faction of the Potawatomi tribe had been involved in movement and migrations for at least two centuries before the trek to Kansas. Like the other Algonkian people in the four-state area surrounding Lake Michigan, the Potawatomis had carried on diplomatic relations with France, Britain, the United States, and other Indian groups on a very pragmatic level. This diplomacy necessitated ongoing mobility that served to relieve internal pressures that might have been more divisive in static circumstances. The real problem, says Clifton, was that in Kansas in the mid-nineteenth century, the traditionalist faction fell victim to a group of land speculators who enjoyed the support of the more acculturated "citizen" faction of the tribe. In his "Factional Conflict and the Indian Community: The Prairie Potawatomi Case" [36], Clifton further argues that specific tribal membership was never very strict or even very important—a circumstance that made it all the more difficult for the Potawatomis to deal with the White land jobbers in Kansas.

To supplement George A. Schultz's biography of Isaac McCoy [155] on the theoretical arguments for removal, the serious student should consult William Miles, "'Enamoured with Colonization': Isaac McCoy's Plan of Indian Reform" [122]. Miles characterized McCoy as an eclectic reformer whose previous work with the American Colonization Society and the plight of the Blacks in general had a significant effect on his designs for removal and for creation of an Indian state in the West. One political aspect of the question is dealt with by William E. Connelley in his "Kansas City, Kansas: Its Place in the History of the State" [41]. With a paucity of documentary evidence, Connelley conjectures that politicians determined to prevent the organization of a free state west of Missouri and that they supported the plan for an Indian state that would prevent implementation of the Missouri Compromise.

A number of articles chronicle the actual removals to the future state of Kansas. Various themes included in these studies are: poor government planning, funding, and administration; the determination of merchants and traders to block removals that would terminate their economic domination of tribal annuities; social and political factionalism; sickness and excessive consumption of alcohol dispensed by White merchants who accompanied the Indians to Kansas; and the dominant role of the mixed-bloods in treaty negotiations, decisions regarding surveys, agricultural assistance, and the allotment of lands in fee simple to selected individual members of the various tribes.

The Potawatomis have attracted the most attention. An old but still important article is "Centennial of Removal of the Potawatomi" [33]. R. David Edmunds has published two scholarly articles, "The Prairie Potawatomie Removal of 1833" [51] and "Potawatomis in the Platte Country: An Indian Removal Incomplete" [52]. Daniel McDonald's article-length book titled *Removal of the Pottawattomie Indians from Northern Indiana* [110] is less informative than Dwight L. Smith's expert edition of "The Attempted Potawatomi Emigration of 1839" [157]. Bert Anson's "Chief Francis Lafontaine and the Miami Emigration from Indiana" [5] is a classic study of the way some Indian leaders made fortunes from removal. Trader chicanery among the Sacs and Foxes is a basic theme in Donald J. Berthrong's "John Beach and the Removal of the Sauk and Fox from Iowa" [19]. Two studies of the Wyandot removal are Ray E.

Merwin, "The Wyandot Indians" [119], and Carl G. Klopfenstein, "The Removal of the Wyandots from Ohio" [99]. Klopfenstein has also written a scholarly study of Shawnee removal in his "Westward Ho: Removal of the Ohio Shawnees, 1832–1833" [100]; another article on the Shawnees is Dorothy V. Jones, "A Preface to the Settlement of Kansas" [94]. C. A. Weslager's *The Delaware Indian Westward Migration, with the Texts of Two Manuscripts (1821–22) Responding to General Lewis Cass's Inquiries about Lenape Culture and Language* [182] provides valuable documentation on the Delaware removal. Important articles on the Iowas and Quapaws are Roy W. Meyer, "The Iowa Indians, 1836–1885" [121], Jack Lane, "Federal-Quapaw Relations, 1800–1833" [102], and W. David Baird, "The Reduction of a People: The Quapaw Removal, 1824–1834" [9].

Several prominent White travelers registered their impressions regarding the prospects of the emigrant Indians in Kansas. Perhaps the most informative and objective are the observations of Henry R. Schoolcraft, whose multivolume *Historical and Statistical Information Respecting the History, Conditions, and Prospects of the Indian Tribes of the United States* [154] contains valuable ethnographic data on some of the Kansas tribes. The Reverend C. B. Boynton and T. B. Mason, representing the "Kansas League of Cincinnati," whose purpose was to promote a White settlement in eastern Kansas, reported in their *A Journey through Kansas; with Sketches of Nebraska: Describing the Country, Climate, Soil, Mineral, Manufacturing and Other Resources. The Results of a Tour Made in the*

Autumn of 1854 [25] that the Wyandots, Delawares, Potawatomis, and Shawnees were in control of strategically located reserves that in the name of Christianity and "civilization" must one day become the property of White people. Horace Greeley, in his *An Overland Journey, from New York to San Francisco in the Summer of 1859* [74], singled out the Delawares and Potawatomis as utterly lazy and degraded. He went on to predict the death of these peoples unless they could be taught the virtues of agriculture and Christianity. Other travelers who agreed with this point of view were George Gale, whose *Upper Mississippi; or, Historical Sketches of the Mound-Builders, the Indian Tribes, and the Progress of Civilization in the North-West; from A.D. 1600 to the Present Time* [63] made no distinction between civilization and Christianity, and C. C. Spalding, whose *Annals of the City of Kansas: Embracing Full Details of the Trade and Commerce of the Great Western Plains* [160] characterized the emigrant tribes as pitiable obstacles to human progress.

The indigenous tribes of Kansas were not unaffected by the arrival of the emigrant Indians. In 1825 both the Osages and the Kansas were encouraged to cede substantial acreage in eastern Kansas to accommodate the Indians from the East. Traditional village sites had to be abandoned in favor of locations that made the Osages and Kansas more vulnerable to attacks by the better-mounted Pawnees, Southern Cheyennes, Southern Arapahos, Kiowas, and Comanches. As competition from the diminishing bison supply became more intense, as whiskey flowed more freely on the overland routes to the Rocky Mountain gold fields, and as epidemic disease became more commonplace, the consequences for all of the tribes were destructive in the extreme. The eruption of the High Plains Indian wars of the early 1860s only aggravated this difficult situation. The standard works on the indigenous tribes are Donald J. Berthrong, *The Southern Cheyennes* [20], Virginia Cole Trenholm, *The Arapahoes, Our People* [164], John Joseph Mathews, *The Osages: Children of the Middle Waters* [117], William E. Unrau, *The Kansa Indians: A History of the Wind People, 1673–1873* [167], Mildred P. Mayhall, *The Kiowas* [118], and Ernest Wallace and E. Adamson Hoebel, *The Comanches: Lords of the Southern Plains* [175]. George E. Hyde's *Pawnee Indians* [90] is informative but lacks the documentation generally expected in modern scholarship.

Indicative of the fact that early state officials were unconcerned with the increasingly destitute condition of the emigrant Indians is the failure of former Kansas governor Samuel J. Crawford to even mention the problem in his *Kansas in the Sixties* [43], which has a good deal to say about his alleged leadership in forcing the Plains tribes to abandon the Jayhawk state. In an important article titled "A Study of the Laws of the Ottawa Indians as Preserved in the OTTAWA FIRST BOOK (1850)" [144], Theodore John Rivers has demonstrated how the Ottawa removal to Kansas resulted in a significant change from customary law to statute law that placed the greatest emphasis on criminal matters as defined by White agents and missionaries. Merchant avarice and early town promotion in Kansas Territory are the subjects of William E. Unrau's "The Council Grove Merchants and Kansa Indians" [166]. That the implicit illegalities of these actions took place under government supervision makes the incident all the more tragic.

By 1846 the nearly two dozen emigrant tribes, aggregating approximately 10,000 persons, had been forcibly settled in the eastern third of the future Kansas. This displacement coincided with what Robert A. Trennert, Jr., has recently termed a major watershed in the evolution of United States Indian policy. In his *Alternative to Extinction: Federal Indian Policy and the Beginnings of the Reservation System, 1846–1851* [165], Trennert effectively demonstrates that a reservation system in the ideal sense — largely the work of Indian commissioners William Medill and Luke Lea — was almost immediately distorted and then destroyed by White land hunger. In the process, the border or emigrant tribes of Kansas were some of the first native Americans to suffer.

Conflict Between Federal Land and Indian Policies

As has been noted in Annie Heloise Abel's "Proposals for an Indian State, 1778–1878" [2], the idea of an Indian state goes back to the Confederation period of United States history. Although Thomas Jefferson, William Crawford, John C. Calhoun, and John Quincy Adams lent some support to the idea, it was Isaac McCoy, Thomas L. McKenney, and especially the Reverend

Jedidiah Morse who were the most active in the movement. A basic problem that continued to block any serious consideration of the measure was legislative fear of too much executive power and discretion over military affairs and administration, and the complaints of tribal leaders that an Indian state would seriously erode their own power. Mounting sectional animosity, particularly after the Nullification crisis of 1832, was an additional obstacle.

Further complicating the issue were a number of late nineteenth and early twentieth century publications that presented a distorted picture of Kansas history during the formative years. In one of the truly classic examples of what professional historians term historiographical misconception, the economic, social, and political crises of the emigrant tribes were for years clouded by the "Bleeding Kansas" interpretation regarding the period immediately preceding the Civil War. Even a casual reading of Charles Robinson, *The Kansas Conflict* [146], Alice Nichols, *Bleeding Kansas* [130], A. T. Andreas, *History of the State of Kansas* [4], William E. Connelley, "The Prairie Band of Pottawatomie Indians (Reservation, Jackson County, Kansas)" [39], and Connelley's five-volume *A Standard History of Kansas and Kansans* [40], suggests that during the seven years preceding Kansas statehood and the beginning of the Civil War of 1861, the paramount problem was a violent conflict between slavemongers, mainly from Missouri, and more virtuous abolitionists from New England and the Midwest. The plight of the emigrant tribes is cast in an extremely minor light (if at all); and, to add insult to injury, Robinson—the first state governor, who was intricately involved in Indian land speculation—refused to record one word regarding the Indians whose land he was determined to secure in fee simple for personal and public profit.

Fortunately, more responsible and professional historians have clarified the basic issues involved. Without dismissing the importance of the slave issue in territorial Kansas, such scholars as James C. Malin, *The Nebraska Question, 1852–1854* [112], Roy Gittinger, "The Separation of Nebraska and Kansas from the Indian Territory" [69], Henry E. Fritz, "George W. Manypenny and *Our Indian Wards*" [60], Homer E. Socolofsky, "How We Took the Land" [158], an unsigned article titled "Wyandot and Shawnee Lands in Wyandotte County, Kansas" [184], H. Craig Miner and William E. Unrau, *The End of Indian Kansas: A Study of Cultural Revolution, 1854–1871* [125], William Frank Zornow, *Kansas: A History of the Jayhawk State* [187], Robert W. Richmond, *Kansas: A Land of Contrasts* [143], and Paul Wallace Gates's monumental *Fifty Million Acres: Conflicts over Kansas Land Policy, 1854–1890* [65] have emphasized the very basic fact that Kansas during the two decades after 1854 was a place where federal land and Indian policies were pulling at cross purposes. On the one hand the government was legally responsible for protecting the interests of the emigrant tribes, while on the other an increasingly permissive land disposal policy and administrative interpretations regarding the Preemption Act of 1841 encouraged White squatters to overrun the Indian reserves with impunity.

Political disruption at the national level is brilliantly analyzed in Roy F. Nichols, "The Kansas-Nebraska Act: A Century of Historiography" [131]. Imre Sutton's *Indian Land Tenure: Bibliographical Essays and a Guide to the Literature* [163] and Jay P. Kinney's *A Continent lost—A Civilization Won: Indian Land Tenure in America* [98] are essential reference works for understanding some of the more perplexing Indian land problems. Political collusion and bureaucratic snarls at the highest levels are explored in "Governor Reeder's Administration" [71], Paul Wallace Gates, "A Fragment of Kansas Land History: The Disposal of the Christian Indian Tract" [64], and Edmund J. Danziger, Jr.'s, *Indians and Bureaucrats: Administering the Reservation Policy during the Civil War* [46]. Early movements toward selected allotments of Indian reserves are described in Paul Wallace Gates, "Indian Allotments Preceding the Dawes Act" [66], and Homer Socolofsky's important appraisal, "Wyandot Floats" [159], in the *Kansas Historical Quarterly.*

George W. Manypenny, Indian commissioner during the Pierce administration, contends in his *Our Indian Wards* [113] that because of White land hunger and ineffectual military support of the Indian Office, the emigrant tribes in Kansas were further on the road to White civilization in 1855 than they were a decade later. The devastating impact of industrial technology and corporate investment in Indian lands is carefully discussed in H. Craig Miner's "Border Frontier: The Missouri River,

Fort Scott & Gulf Railroad in the Cherokee Neutral Lands, 1868–1870" [123] and in his *The Corporation and the Indian: Tribal Sovereignty and Industrial Civilization in Indian Territory, 1865–1907* [124]. The disruption occasioned by the Civil War upon federal Indian policy and administration resulted in the flight of nearly seven thousand "Union" Indians from the Indian Territory to Kansas. This and related problems are dealt with in Dean Banks, "Civil War Refugees from Indian Territory in the North" [11], W. David Baird, *The Quapaw People* [10], Edmund J. Danziger, Jr., "The Office of Indian Affairs and the Problem of Civil War Refugees in Kansas" [45], and Harry Kelsey, "William P. Dole and Mr. Lincoln's Indian Policy" [97].

Tribal Leadership and Factional Response

As more and more removal treaties were negotiated in the 1850s and 1860s, leaders of the various tribes were placed under enormous pressure by agents from Washington, well-organized squatter organizations in Kansas, and leaders of the American business community. Bribery, duplicity, legalistically phrased articles in the various treaties, and vacillating congressional responses contributed to the aggravation of factionalism that in many cases had plagued the emigrants before their arrival in Kansas.

Perhaps the best general introduction to factionalism and tribal leadership is P. Richard Metcalf,

"Who Should Rule at Home? Native American Politics and Indian-White Relations" [120]. Using as one of his examples the Blackhawk-Keokuk feud among the Sacs and Foxes that continued after some factions of these people came to Kansas, Metcalf emphasizes that political feuding was as common among native Americans as among White people. He makes a special plea for more accurate research into the entire problem. In a similar vein, James A. Clifton, in "Factional Conflict and the Indian Community: The Prairie Potawatomi Case" [36], emphasizes the loose and subjective character of tribal organization before extensive White contact. In his "Potawatomi Indians of the West: Origins of the Citizens Band" [128], Joseph Francis Murphy points to widespread intermarriages with Whites and members of other tribes, as well as the influence of Jesuit missionaries, in separating the "Citizens Band" from the traditionalists. Similar conclusions have been documented by Dorothy V. Jones, "A Potawatomi Faces the Problem of Cultural Change: Joseph N. Bourassa in Kansas" [95].

Three interesting narratives by Charles R. Green, an early White settler on the Sac and Fox reservation, provide additional information regarding factionalism and tribal leaders. *Early Days in Kansas, Pioneer Narratives of the First Twenty-five Years of Kansas History* [75], *Early Days in Kansas, in Keokuks Time on the Kansas Reservation* [76], and *Sac and Fox Indians in Kansas* [77] describe how the government paid some chiefs up to $500 a year for their cooperation in policies designed to destroy tribal cohesion. Even though Green was biased in favor of Christian missionaries and the White man with the plow, he decried the ultimate tragedy of divided leadership. An excellent example of a badly divided tribal fragment that finally was forced from Canada to Kansas is C. A. Weslager's description of the refugee Delaware-Munsies, in "Enrollment List of Chippewa and Delaware-Munsies Living in Franklin County, Kansas, May 31, 1900" [181].

The unusual deference granted mixed-blood leaders Charles Journeycake among the Delawares, Silas Armstrong and William Walker among the Wyandots, and Francis Lafontaine among the Miamis is assessed in, respectively, Harry M. Roark, *Charles Journeycake: Indian Statesman and Christian Leader* [145], Orin J. Oliphant, ed., "The Report of the Wyandot Exploring Delegation, 1831" [134], and Bert Anson, "Variations of the Indian Conflict: The Effects of the Emigrant Indian Removal Policy, 1830–1854" [6]. How a combination of land speculators, internal factionalism, epidemic disease, missionary activity, and government duplicity virtually obliterated one of the major Kansas tribes is the subject of William E. Unrau, "Removal, Death, and Legal Reincarnation of the Kaw People" [172]. The same author's "The Mixed-Blood Connection: Charles Curtis and Kaw Detribalization" [171] suggests how one enterprising mixed-blood caught between contending cultures used his one-eighth native American gene quantum to good political advantage, including selection as the first Indian vice-president of the United States. Berlin B.

Chapman's *The Otoes and Missourias: A Study of Indian Removal and the Legal Aftermath* [35] is one of the more sophisticated studies of how expert legal research and interpretation of "Indianness" can determine the political and financial status of a tribe whose land claims in Kansas and elsewhere had been ignored for generations.

W. David Baird, *The Osage People* [8] and *The Quapaw People* [10], Joseph H. Cash, *The Potawatomie People (Citizen Band)* [30], Joseph H. Cash and Gerald W. Wolff, *The Ottawa People* [31], R. David Edmunds, *The Otoe-Missouri People* [53], George R. Nielson, *The Kickapoo People* [133], and William E. Unrau, *The Kaw People* [170] are short but well-researched volumes designed for the general reader as well as the specialist. All emphasize in varying degrees the twentieth-century consequences of factionalism and changing political leadership dating back to the beginnings of recorded history.

Role of the Missionaries

In terms of White cultural imperialism, no one group played a more important role than the Christian missionaries. This is especially evident in Kansas, where the government's plan to "civilize" native Americans had high priority indeed. Although confined to the activities of the Protestant missionaires, the standard work is Robert F. Berkhofer, Jr., *Salvation and the Savage: An Analysis of Protestant Missions and American Indian*

Response, 1787–1862 [16]. In view of the cultural assumptions of the contending groups, it is Berkhofer's reasonable conclusion that general missionary failure was a foregone conclusion, while the converted Indians came to be alienated from Indians and Whites alike. Another solid study of the Protestant effort is R. Pierce Beaver, *Church, State, and the American Indians: Two and a Half Centuries of Partnership in Missions between Protestant Churches and Government* [15]. Although somewhat uncritical of interdenominational bickering over tribal domination, Beaver provides valuable information on the relationships between the various missionary societies and the government's removal policy.

The Shawnee Mission, situated in Kansas just south of the mouth of the Kansas (or Kaw) River, was the one most important mission in all of Kansas. Although less significant than the Methodist church, other Protestant groups maintained stations there as well. The coming of the Civil War prompted a profound division between the Northern Methodists and the emerging Methodist Episcopal Church South. Inevitably, this cleavage created confusion not only among the Shawnees, but among other tribes whom the Methodists were ostensibly attempting to "civilize" with government assistance. The best account of this mission is Martha B. Caldwell, ed., *Annals of the Shawnee Methodist Mission and Indian Manual Training School* [27], which covers the years 1839–65. The more important themes Caldwell emphasizes are the break between the Northern and Southern churches, how the emigrant tribes became almost hopelessly enmeshed in the slavery question, the profiteering of the mission superintendents, and the economic exploitation of Indian children who literally had a cultural revolution forced upon them. Valuable also is James Anderson, "The Methodist Shawnee Mission in Johnson County, Kansas, 1830–1862" [3]. Henry Harvey, a missionary for the Society of Friends, in his *History of the Shawnee Indians, from the Year 1681 to 1854, Inclusive* [84], describes the techniques whereby White male Southerners married Shawnee women as a means of gaining political, economic, and religious influence with the tribe. Informative but biased in favor of the Methodists, are J. J. Lutz, "The Methodist Missions among the Indian Tribes in Kansas" [103], Edith Connelley Ross, "The Old Shawnee Mission" [150], and the Reverend Joab Spencer, "The Shawnee Indians: Their Customs, Traditions and Folk-lore" [161]. Grant W. Harrington's *The Shawnees in Kansas* [83] provides a summary of the trek from Ohio and Missouri to Kansas and explains how "White" Shawnees working with the missionaries viewed the cession and allotment of the Shawnee reservation as virtually inevitable. In a series of reports written mainly in the late 1840s by the Methodist William Johnson to eastern religious journals such as the *Christian Advocate and Journal* and the *Western Christian Advocate,* and reprinted in "Letters from the Indian Missions in Kansas" [93], may be found the details of mission activity among the Shawnees, Delawares, Peorias, Weas, Kansas, and Kickapoos. In general these reports are pessimistic, particularly with regard to the language barrier and the failure of the Indians to take interest in week-long revivals. Equally unsuccessful were the efforts of the United Foreign Missionary Society among the Osages at Mission Neosho, the first mission in Kansas (1824), as described in T. F. Morrison, "Mission Neosho: The First Kansas Mission" [127].

Like the Methodists, the Baptists were active among a number of the tribes, including the Delawares, Potawatomis, and Ottawas. And like their fellow Protestants they emphasized language instruction, manual training, and the virtues of the White man's conception of God. Their recognized leader was Isaac McCoy, whose diverse career has been well documented in George A. Schultz, *An Indian Canaan: Isaac McCoy and the Vision of an Indian State* [155]. Bessie Ellen Moore, "Life and Work of Robert Simerwell" [126], is a scholarly study of one of McCoy's close associates who became a specialist in the Potawatomi language and developed an orthography that was of some help to the missionary endeavor. But in general the Baptist effort was unsuccessful, as Thomas P. Barr, "The Pottawatomie Baptist Manual Labor Training School" [12], and Clara Gowing, "Life among the Delaware Indians" [72], emphasize. M. M. Marberry's *The Golden Voice: A Biography of Isaac Kalloch* [114] is an interesting study of a prominent Baptist minister who, before becoming mayor of San Francisco, engaged in Ottawa land and town speculation and played a crucial role in the Baptist effort to secure control of the Ottawa Indian University.

The somewhat greater success experienced by the

Jesuits was in large measure a consequence of Catholic conversions accomplished before the removal to Kansas. Christian Hoecken's "Father Hoecken's Diary" [85], for example, points out that the arrival of nearly a hundred Catholic Potawatomis at the Sugar Creek Mission near the Missouri border had a very important effect on future success at the later Saint Paul and Saint Mary's missions. That the Jesuits kept not only careful baptism data but detailed records regarding disease, agriculture, commerce, tribal politics, languages, and ethnology may be seen in such works as Arthur Thomas Donohue, "A History of the Early Jesuit Missions in Kansas" [49], Maurice Gailland, "Early Years at St. Mary's Pottowatomie Mission: From the Diary of Father Maurice Gailland, S.J." [62], and W. W. Graves, *Life and Letters of Fathers Ponziglione, Schoemakers, and Other Early Jesuits at Osage Mission* [73]. A disillusioned Reverend Joseph Romig describes the problems at the Chippewa and Munsee reserve in "The Chippewa and Munsee (or Christian) Indians of Franklin County, Kansas" [149], and William E. Connelley, "Religious Conceptions of the Modern Hurons" [42], decries the inability of the mixed-blood Huron-Wyandots to wholly abandon some of their traditional religious practices in the twentieth century.

The generally sorry state of affairs of the various Christian missions at a time when the vast majority of the emigrant tribes had been or were being forced to accept more concentrated reserves in the future Oklahoma is summarized by William Nicholson, "A Tour of

Indian Agencies in Kansas and the Indian Territory in 1870" [132]. Nicholson blamed the government as much as the churches for the small number of firm converts. What he failed to emphasize was that by land speculation, town promotion, and active participation in the restructuring of tribal governments, and in the general movement toward allotment, the missionaries had in fact contributed substantially to cultural change among the emigrant Indians of Kansas.

Impact of Malnutrition, Disease, and Alcohol

The absence of a general study on native American population enumerations for the emigrant tribes covering their residence in Kansas (roughly 1835–75) should not be taken to imply population stability. Henry R. Schoolcraft's mid-nineteenth-century *Historical and Statistical Information Respecting the History, Conditions, and Prospects of the Indian Tribes of the United States* [154], which was commissioned by Congress, is of some help, as are the various *Annual Reports* of the commissioners of Indian affairs. These *Annual Reports,* however, were mainly drawn from the alleged enumerations of the various tribal agents, who often engaged in not-so-educated guessing or simply reported the erroneous counts of their predecessors. Not until 1890 did the federal census-takers make an effort to count native Americans with some degree of accuracy. But that the emigrant tribes experienced profound population losses during their four-decade sojourn in Kansas is clearly apparent from the modest amount of data that has been analyzed. For the complex problems involved in the general study of native American population trends, the serious student should consult Henry F. Dobyns's expert appraisal of the literature in *Native American Historical Demography: A Critical Bibliography* [48].

Most of the emigrant tribes negotiated some form of land cession treaties before they arrived in Kansas — treaties that in most instances promised annuities designed to sustain them during the period of time calculated by the government as needed for the transition to White "civilization." Seldom were these annuities paid on schedule; and, when they were, the clever and eager hands of traders, speculators, certain missionaries, government agents, and even tribal leaders took more than their fair share. Too often the result was malnutrition, a consequent susceptibility to the ravages of various diseases, or even outright starvation. Solid tribal ethnohistories that stress these tragedies in their varying historical contexts are: Bert Anson, *The Miami Indians* [7]; Alan W. Farley, *The Delaware Indians in Kansas, 1829–1867* [55]; Arrell M. Gibson, *The Kickapoos: Lords of the Middle Border* [67]; William T. Hagan, *The Sac and Fox Indians* [78]; John Joseph Mathews, *The Osages: Children of the Middle Waters* [117]; William E. Unrau, *The Kansa Indians: A History of the Wind People, 1673–1873* [167]; and C. A. Weslager, *The Delaware Indians: A History* [180]. H. Craig Miner and William E. Unrau take a hard look at the problem on a topical basis in *The End of Indian Kansas: A Study of Cultural Revolution, 1854–1871* [125].

Waldo R. Wedel's "The Kansa Indians" [179] provides a general survey of the sources for determining population enumerations for one of the major Kansas tribes.

Even though there is a paucity of careful studies of epidemic disease among the individual emigrant tribes, there is enough general information to conclude that smallpox, cholera, and various bronchial and intestinal maladies took a frightening number of lives in the middle half of the nineteenth century. Wildlife diseases played a fatal role as well. As a general introduction to the problem the reader should consult Alfred W. Crosby, Jr., *The Columbian Exchange: Biological and Cultural Consequences of 1492* [44], and Calvin Martin, "Wildlife Diseases as a Factor in the Depopulation of the North American Indian" [115].

Because most of the emigrant tribes who came to Kansas once resided in the eastern part of North America, where the vicious smallpox epidemics accompanying the colonial wars of the seventeenth and eighteenth centuries took their deadly toll, it is important to remember that oral accounts of these devastating events handed down to subsequent generations in the nineteenth century played a significant role in the attitudes of the Kansas tribes as they experienced new invasions of their only recently awarded reservations. At least three major smallpox epidemics hit the native Americans during their residence in Kansas: one in 1832–33, another in 1836, and an extremely devastating one during the years 1852–56. Specific tribes known to have been especially afflicted and that in some instances experienced a fatality rate of up to 30 percent were the Potawatomis, Kickapoos, Sacs and Foxes, Delawares, Kansas, and Osages. Cholera also took its toll, especially in the wake of the vast movement of gold-seekers to California across northeastern Kansas at midcentury, and there is some evidence that this disease irrupted in Kansas as early as 1833. Louise Barry's *The Beginning of the West* [13] and her "The Kansa Indians and the Census of 1843" [14] provide scattered data, as does E. Wagner Stearn and Allen E. Stearn, *The Effect of Smallpox on the Destiny of the Amerindian* [162]. Thomas P. Barr, "The Pottawatomie Baptist Manual Labor Training School" [12], and Bessie Ellen Moore, "Life and Work of Robert Simerwell" [126], are examples of how church officials recorded epidemic data in a reasonably objective manner. William E. Unrau, "The Depopulation of the Dheghia-Siouan Kansa prior to Removal" [169], uses a variety of documents to indicate how a combination of smallpox, cholera, and malnutrition played the major role in reducing the population of the Kansa tribe by more than 60 percent in less than two generations.

Virtually every report from the various Indian agencies in Kansas complained to Washington officialdom about the illicit sale and distribution of intoxicating beverages to the emigrant tribes. In the summer of 1841, for example, eight thousand gallons of "common whiskey" moved past the Shawnee Baptist Mission near the mouth of the Kaw. One agent reported that same year that every other house on the western boundary of Missouri was in one way or another involved in the distribution of alcohol to the Indians. Fatalities and irrational agreements made at treaty conferences by intoxicated native American leaders were depressingly commonplace. Even the passage of more stringent federal legislation in 1847 — providing for heavy prison penalties for offenders and allowing Indians to serve as competent witnesses in whiskey trials — helped very little. The profits were simply too attractive, not enough federal troops were available to enforce the law, and with the formal opening of the Kansas Territory in 1854 and the increase of reservation cessions that provided White squatters at least a quasi-legal title to former Indian land in the Territory, so-called dram shops could be found at the edge of all the diminished reservations. The standard study of this incredible tragedy is Otto F. Frederickson, *The Liquor Question among the Indian Tribes in Kansas, 1804–1881* [59]. In the 1880s, after most of the emigrant Indians had been relocated in the future Oklahoma, a feeble and unconvincing attempt was made by W. H. Johnson, "The Saloon in Indian Territory" [92], to argue that whiskey was no longer a major problem in Indian Territory; this was effectively refuted by Gail Hamilton in his "Prisoner among the Indians" [79]. In terms of depopulation and cultural destruction, the illegal sale of alcohol to the emigrant tribes was certainly as important as malnutrition and epidemic disease.

Expulsion from Kansas

Kansas became the thirty-fourth state in the same year that the American Civil War tore the Union asunder. One year later, on 20 May 1862, a Homestead Law was passed by a Republican-dominated Congress that opened the floodgates of White farmer penetration into the trans-Missouri West. Less than two months later, on 1 July, the same Congress authorized the construction of a central transcontinental railroad that would receive massive government loans and, more important for native Americans in Kansas, railroad rights-of-way and adjacent land grants amounting to five alternating 640-acre sections of land for every mile of track constructed. These actions and laws sealed the doom of the emigrant tribes, who since the organization of the Kansas Territory in 1854 had been subjected to degradation and removal pressures seldom equaled in native American history. By the early 1870s, in terms of a biological as opposed to a social definition of an Indian, approximately one thousand emigrant Indians remained in Kansas. These were mainly the traditionalist factions of the Potawatomis and Kickapoos, a few Sacs and Foxes, and an even smaller number of Iowas. An assortment of largely enculturated mixed-bloods, of course, continued to reside in the new thirty-fourth state as individual property owners and supporters of the new disposition. It was indeed a revolutionary state of affairs.

Professional studies on the Civil War, the Homestead

Act, and the Pacific Railroad Bill are beyond the scope of this bibliography. Important, however, in understanding the gallery of Kansas politicians who played a large role in dispossessing the emigrant tribes during the Civil War is Albert Castel, *A Frontier State at War: Kansas, 1861–1865* [32]. H. Craig Miner's *The Corporation and the Indian: Tribal Sovereignty and Industrial Civilization in Indian Territory, 1865–1907* [124] is the most carefully researched analysis of post–Civil War economic exploitation of native Americans who were finally dispatched to Indian Territory. Grant Foreman, *The Last Trek of the Indians* [58], recounts some of the factors leading to the removals from Kansas, but the most interpretive appraisal of the moral and legal questions involved is H. Craig Miner and William E. Unrau, *The End of Indian Kansas: A Study of Cultural Revolution, 1854–1871* [125]. Berlin B. Chapman, "Removal of the Osages from Kansas" [34], recounts the legal machinations involved in one tribe's removal, while Ruth Landes, *The Prairie Potawatomi: Tradition and Ritual in the Twentieth Century* [101], and J. Neale Carman and Karl S. Pond in "The Replacement of the Indian Languages of Kansas by English" [29], deal with the destruction of native linguistic skills resulting from the final removal from Kansas.

Those interested in the politics and economic forces dictating that the future Oklahoma be the setting where the emigrant tribes would finally experience the full force of the government's plan of detribalization should consult Duane Gage, "Oklahoma: A Resettlement Area for Indians" [61], and Roy Gittinger, *The Formation of the State of Oklahoma (1803–1906)* [68]. Finally, it should be emphasized that on the subject of this bibliographical critique, a vast amount of virgin manuscript material in the National Archives and various regional depositories remains to be critically analyzed.

ALPHABETICAL LIST AND INDEX

* Denotes items suitable for secondary school students.

Item
no.

Essay
page
no.

[1] Abel, Annie Heloise. 1908. "The History of Events Resulting in Indian Consolidation West of the Mississippi." In *Annual Report of the American Historical Association for the Year 1906,* 1:233–450. Washington, D.C. (7)

[2] ———. 1908. "Proposals for an Indian State, 1778–1878." In *Annual Report of the American Historical Association for the Year 1907,* 1:87–104. Washington, D.C. (7, 24)

[3] Anderson, James. 1956. "The Methodist Shawnee Mission in Johnson County, Kansas, 1830–1862." *Trail Guide* 1 (January): 7–20. (33)

[4] Andreas, A. T. 1883. *History of the State of Kansas.* Chicago: Alfred T. Andreas. (25)

[5] Anson, Bert. 1964. "Chief Francis Lafontaine and the Miami Emigration from Indiana." *Indiana Magazine of History* 60:241–68. (20)

[6] ———. 1964. "Variations of the Indian Conflict: The Effects of the Emigrant Indian Removal Policy, 1830–1854." *Missouri Historical Review* 59:64–89. (17, 30)

[7] ———. 1970. *The Miami Indians.* Norman: University of Oklahoma Press. (37)

[8] Baird, W. David. 1972. *The Osage People.* Phoenix: Indian Tribal Series. (31)

[9] ———. 1974. "The Reduction of a People: The Quapaw Removal, 1824–1834." *Red River Valley Historical Review* 1:21–36. (21)

[10] ———. 1975. *The Quapaw People.* Phoenix: Indian Tribal Series. (28, 31)

[11] Banks, Dean. 1963. "Civil War Refugees from Indian Territory in the North." *Chronicles of Oklahoma* 41:286–98. (28)

[12] Barr, Thomas P. 1977. "The Pottawatomie Baptist Manual Labor Training School." *Kansas Historical Quarterly* 43:377–431. (34, 39)

[13] Barry, Louise. 1972. *The Beginning of the West*. Topeka: Kansas State Historical Society. (15, 39)

[14] ———. 1973. "The Kansa Indians and the Census of 1843." *Kansas Historical Quarterly* 39:478–90. (39)

[15] Beaver, Robert Pierce. 1966. *Church, State, and the American Indians: Two and a Half Centuries of Partnership in Missions between Protestant Churches and Government*. Saint Louis: Concordia Publishing House. (32)

[16] Berkhofer, Robert F., Jr. 1965. *Salvation and the Savage; An Analysis of Protestant Missions and American Indian Response, 1787–1862*. Lexington: University of Kentucky Press. (32)

[17] ———. 1971. "The Political Context of a New Indian History." *Pacific Historical Review* 40:357–82. (5)

[18]   ———. 1978. *The White Man's Indian: Images of the American Indian from Columbus to the Present.* New York: Alfred A. Knopf.   (ix)

[19]   Berthrong, Donald J. 1956. "John Beach and the Removal of the Sauk and Fox from Iowa." *Iowa Journal of History* 54:313–34.   (8, 20)

[20]   ———. 1963. *The Southern Cheyennes.* Norman: University of Oklahoma Press.   (23)

[21]   Blair, Emma Helen, ed. 1911–12. *The Indian Tribes of the Upper Mississippi Valley and Region of the Great Lakes.* 2 vols. Cleveland: Arthur H. Clark Company.   (3)

[22]   Blumenthal, Walter H. 1955. *American Indians Dispossessed: Fraud in Land Cessions Forced upon the Tribes.* Philadelphia: George S. MacManus Company.   (5)

[23]   Bond, Beverly W., Jr. 1934. *The Civilization of the Old Northwest.* New York: Macmillan Company.   (2)

[24]   Bourassa, J. N. 1972. "The Life of
        Wah-bahn-se: The Warrior Chief of the
        Pottawatamies." *Kansas Historical Quar-
        terly* 38:132–43.   (ix)

[25]   Boynton, Rev. Charles B., and T. B.
        Mason, 1855. *A Journey through Kansas;
        with Sketches of Nebraska: Describing the
        Country, Climate, Soil, Mineral, Manufac-
        turing and Other Resources. The Results of a
        Tour Made in the Autumn of 1854.*
        Cincinnati: Moore, Wilstach, Keys.   (22)

[26]   Buley, Roscoe Carlyle. 1950. *The Old
        Northwest: Pioneer Period, 1815–1840.* 2
        vols. Indianapolis: Indiana Historical
        Society.   (2)

[27]   Caldwell, Martha B., ed. 1939. *Annals of
        the Shawnee Methodist Mission and Indian
        Manual Training School.* Topeka: Kansas
        State Historical Society.   (32)

[28]   Callendar, Charles, 1962. *Social Organ-
        ization of the Central Algonkian Indians.*
        Publications in Anthropology, no. 7.
        Milwaukee: Milwaukee Public Museum.   (4)

[29]   Carman, J. Neale, and Karl S. Pond.
        1955. "The Replacement of the Indian
        Languages of Kansas by English." *Trans-
        actions of the Kansas Academy of Science*
        58:131–50.   (42)

[30]   Cash, Joseph H. 1976. *The Potawatomi
        People (Citizen Band)*. Phoenix: Indian
        Tribal Series.   (31)

[31]   Cash, Joseph H., and Gerald W. Wolff.
        1976. *The Ottawa People*. Phoenix: In-
        dian Tribal Series.   (31)

[32]   Castel, Albert. 1958. *A Frontier State at
        War: Kansas, 1861–1865*. Ithaca: Cor-
        nell University Press.   (42)

[33]   "Centennial of Removal of the
        Potawatomi." 1938. *Indiana History
        Bulletin* 15 (August): 285–86.   (20)

[34]   Chapman, Berlin B. 1938. "Removal of
        the Osages from Kansas." *Kansas Histori-
        cal Quarterly* 7:287–305, 399–410.   (42)

[35]   ———. 1965. *The Otoes and Missourias: A Study of Indian Removal and the Legal Aftermath.* Oklahoma City: Times Journal Publishing Company.   (31)

[36]   Clifton, James A. 1968. "Factional Conflict and the Indian Community: The Prairie Potawatomi Case." In *The American Indian Today,* ed. Stuart Levine and Nancy O. Lurie, pp. 115–32. Deland, Florida: Everett/ Edwards. Paperback reprint, Baltimore: Penguin, 1972.   (19, 29)

[37]   ———. 1970. "Chicago Was Theirs." *Chicago History* 1:5–17.   (18)

[38]   ———. 1977. *The Prairie People: Continuity and Change in Potawatomi Indian Culture, 1665–1965.* Lawrence: Regents Press of Kansas.   (9, 18)

[39]   Connelley, William E. 1915–18. "The Prairie Band of Pottawatomie Indians (Reservation, Jackson County, Kansas)." *Collections of the Kansas State Historical Society* 14:488–570.   (25)

[40]   ———. 1918. *A Standard History of Kansas and Kansans.* 5 vols. Chicago: Lewis Publishing Company.   (25)

[41]   ———. 1919–22. "Kansas City, Kansas: Its Place in the History of the State." *Collections of the Kansas State Historical Society* 15:181–91.   (19)

[42]   ———. 1919–22. "Religious Conceptions of the Modern Hurons." *Collections of the Kansas State Historical Society* 15:92–102.   (35)

[43]   Crawford, Samuel J. 1911. *Kansas in the Sixties.* Chicago: A. C. McClurg.   (23)

[44]   Crosby, Alfred W., Jr. 1972. *The Columbian Exchange: Biological and Cultural Consequences of 1492.* Westport, Conn.: Greenwood Press.   (38)

[45]   Danziger, Edmund J., Jr. 1969. "The Office of Indian Affairs and the Problem of Civil War Refugees in Kansas." *Kansas Historical Quarterly* 35:257–75.   (28)

[46]   ———. 1974. *Indians and Bureaucrats: Administering the Reservation Policy during the Civil War.* Urbana: University of Illinois Press.   (27)

[47]   DeRosier, Arthur H., Jr. 1970. *The Removal of the Choctaw Indians.* Knoxville: University of Tennessee Press.   (9)

[48]   Dobyns, Henry F. 1976. *Native American Historical Demography: A Critical Bibliography.* Newberry Library Center for the History of the American Indian Bibliographical Series. Bloomington: Indiana University Press.   (37)

[49]   Donohue, Arthur Thomas. 1940. "A History of the Early Jesuit Missions in Kansas." Ph.D. diss., University of Kansas.   (35)

[50]   Eblen, Jack E. 1968. *The First and Second United States Empires: Governors and Territorial Government, 1784–1912.* Pittsburgh: University of Pittsburgh Press.   (2)

[51]   Edmunds, R. David. 1972. "The Prairie
        Potawatomi Removal of 1833." *Indiana
        Magazine of History* 68:240–53.   (20)

[52]   ———. 1974. "Potawatomis in the Platte
        County: An Indian Removal Incom-
        plete." *Missouri Historical Review*
        68:375–92.   (20)

[53]   ———. 1976. *The Otoe-Missouri People.*
        Phoenix: Indian Tribal Series.   (31)

[54]   ———. 1978. *The Powatatomis: Keepers of
        the Fire.* Norman: University of Okla-
        homa Press.   (4)

[55]   Farley, Alan W. 1955. *The Delaware In-
        dians in Kansas, 1829–1867.* Kansas City,
        Kans. n.p.   (37)

[56]   Fisher, Robert L. 1933. "The Treaties of
        Portage des Sioux." *Mississippi Valley His-
        torical Review* 19:495–508.   (4)

[57]   Folmer, Henri. 1953. *Franco-Spanish
        Rivalry in North America, 1524–1763.*
        Glendale, Calif.: Arthur H. Clark Com-
        pany.   (15)

[58]*   Foreman, Grant. 1946. *The Last Trek of
        the Indians*. Chicago: University of
        Chicago Press. Reprinted, N.Y.: Russell
        and Russell, 1972.   (18, 42)

[59]   Frederikson, Otto F. 1932. *The Liquor
        Question among the Indian Tribes in Kansas,
        1804–1881*. Bulletin of the University
        of Kansas, Humanistic Studies, vol. 4,
        no. 4. Lawrence: University of Kansas
        Department of Journalism Press.   (40)

[60]   Fritz, Henry E. 1971. "George W. Man-
        ypenny and *Our Indian Wards.*" *Kansas
        Quarterly* 3:100–104.   (26)

[61]   Gage, Duane. 1969. "Oklahoma: A Re-
        settlement Area for Indians." *Chronicles
        of Oklahoma* 47:282–97.   (43)

[62]   Gailland, Maurice. 1953. "Early Years at
        St. Mary's Pottowatomie Mission: From
        the Diary of Father Maurice Gailland,
        S.J.," ed. James M. Burke. *Kansas Histor-
        ical Quarterly* 20:501–29.   (35)

[63]   Gale, George. 1867. *Upper Mississippi; or,
        Historical Sketches of the Mound-Builders,*

*the Indian Tribes, and the Progress of Civili-
zation in the North-West; from A.D. 1600 to
the Present Time.* Chicago: Clarke.   (22)

[64]   Gates, Paul Wallace. 1937. "A Fragment
of Kansas Land History: The Disposal
of the Christian Indian Tract." *Kansas
Historical Quarterly* 6:227–40.   (27)

[65]   ———. 1954. *Fifty Million Acres: Conflicts
over Kansas Land Policy, 1854–1890.*
Ithaca: Cornell University Press.   (26)

[66]   ———. 1971. "Indian Allotments Pre-
ceding the Dawes Act." In *The Frontier
Challenge: Responses to the Trans-
Mississippi West,* ed. John G. Clark, pp.
141–70. Lawrence: University Press of
Kansas.   (27)

[67]   Gibson, Arrell M. 1963. *The Kickapoos:
Lords of the Middle Border.* Norman: Uni-
versity of Oklahoma Press.   (37)

[68]   Gittinger, Roy. 1917. *The Formation of the
State of Oklahoma (1803–1906).* Ber-

keley: University of California Press. 2d
ed., Norman: University of Oklahoma
Press, 1939. (43)

[69] ———. 1917. "The Separation of Ne-
braska and Kansas from the Indian
Territory." *Mississippi Valley Historical
Review* 3:442–61. (26)

[70] Gordon, Leon M., II. 1950. "The Red
Man's Retreat from Northern Indiana."
Indiana Magazine of History 46:39–60. (4)

[71] "Governor Reeder's Administration."
1889–96. *Transactions of the Kansas State
Historical Society* 5:163–234. (27)

[72] Gowing, Clara. 1911–12. "Life among
the Delaware Indians." *Collections of the
Kansas State Historical Society* 12:183–93. (34)

[73] Graves, W. W. 1916. *Life and Letters of
Fathers Ponziglione, Schoemakers, and
Other Early Jesuits at Osage Mission.* Saint
Paul, Kans.: W. W. Graves. (35)

[74] Greeley, Horace. 1860. *An Overland
Journey, from New York to San Francisco in*

the Summer of 1859. New York: C. M. Saxton, Barker. Republished with notes and an intro. Charles T. Duncan, ed. N.Y.: Knopf, 1964. (22)

[75] Green, Charles R. 1912. *Early Days in Kansas, Pioneer Narratives of the First Twenty-five Years of Kansas History.* Olathe, Kans.: Published by the author. (29)

[76] ———. 1913. *Early Days in Kansas, in Keokuks Time on the Kansas Reservation.* Olathe, Kans.: Published by the author. (29)

[77] ———. 1914. *Sac and Fox Indians in Kansas.* Olathe, Kans.: Published by the author. (29)

[78] Hagan, William T. 1958, *The Sac and Fox Indians.* Norman: University of Oklahoma Press. (37)

[79] Hamilton, Gail. 1888. "Prisoner among the Indians." *North American Review* 146:55–56. (40)

[80]   *Handbook of American Indians North of Mexico.* 1907–10. Frederick W. Hodge, ed. 2 vols. Bureau of American Ethnology Bulletin 30. Washington, D.C.: Government Printing Office. Reprinted, N.Y.: Pageant Books, 1959. Other reprints available.   (3)

[81]   *Handbook of North American Indians.* 1978—. William C. Sturtevant, gen. ed. 20 vols. Washington, D.C.: Government Printing Office.   (3)

[82]   Harmon, George Dewey. 1941. *Sixty Years of Indian Affairs, Political, Economic, and Diplomatic, 1789–1850.* Chapel Hill: University of North Carolina Press.   (9)

[83]   Harrington, Grant W. 1937. *The Shawnees in Kansas.* Kansas City, Kans.: Western Pioneer Press.   (33)

[84]   Harvey, Henry. 1855. *History of the Shawnee Indians, from the Year 1681 to 1854, Inclusive.* Cincinnati: Ephraim Morgan and Sons.   (33)

[85]   Hoecken, Christian. 1890. "Father
        Hoecken's Diary." *The Dial* (Saint Mary's
        College, Kansas) 1, no. 4:1–3; 2, no.
        1:1–5; 2, no. 2:17–18; 2, no. 3:35–36.   (35)

[86]   Hollon, W. Eugene. 1966. *The Great
        American Desert: Then and Now.* New
        York: Oxford University Press.   (16)

[87]   Horsman, Reginald. 1967. *Expansion
        and American Indian Policy, 1783–1812.*
        East Lansing: Michigan State University
        Press.   (2)

[88]   ———. 1970. *The Origins of Indian Re-
        moval, 1815–1824.* East Lansing: Michi-
        gan State University Press.   (8)

[89]   ———. 1975. "Scientific Racism and the
        American Indian in the Mid-nineteenth
        Century." *American Quarterly* 27:152–68.   (6)

[90]   Hyde, George E. 1934. The *Pawnee In-
        dians.* 2 vols. Denver: J. Van Male. Re-
        printed, Denver: University of Denver
        Press, 1951; New ed., Norman: Univer-
        sity of Oklahoma Press, 1974.   (23)

[91]   Jahoda, Gloria. 1975. *The Trail of Tears.*
       New York: Holt, Rinehart and Winston.   (18)

[92]   Johnson, W. H. 1888. "The Saloon in
       Indian Territory." *North American Review*
       146:340–41.   (40)

[93]   Johnson, William, and others. 1923–25.
       "Letters from the Indian Missions in
       Kansas." *Collections of the Kansas State His-
       torical Society* 16:227–71.   (33)

[94]   Jones, Dorothy V. 1963. "A Preface to
       the Settlement of Kansas." *Kansas Histor-
       ical Quarterly* 29:122–36.   (21)

[95]   ———. 1971. "A Potawatomi Faces the
       Problem of Cultural Change: Joseph N.
       Bourassa in Kansas." *Kansas Quarterly*
       3:47–55.   (29)

[96]   Kappler, Charles J., comp. 1904. *Indian
       Affairs: Laws and Treaties.* Vol. 2. *Treaties.*
       Washington: Government Printing
       Office. Reprinted with a new foreword by
       Brantley Blue, ed. N.Y.: Interland,
       1975.   (viii)

[97]   Kelsey, Harry. 1971. "William P. Dole and Mr. Lincoln's Indian Policy." *Journal of the West* 10:484–92.   (28)

[98]   Kinney, Jay P. 1937. *A Continent Lost —A Civilization Won: Indian Land Tenure in America.* Baltimore: Johns Hopkins University Press.   (27)

[99]   Klopfenstein, Carl G. 1957. "The Removal of the Wyandots from Ohio." *Ohio Historical Quarterly* 66:119–36.   (21)

[100]   ———. 1957. "Westward Ho: Removal of the Ohio Shawnees, 1832–1833." *Bulletin of the Historical and Philosophical Society of Ohio* 15:3–31.   (21)

[101]   Landes, Ruth. 1970. *The Prairie Potawatomi: Tradition and Ritual in the Twentieth Century.* Madison: University of Wisconsin Press.   (42)

[102]   Lane, Jack. 1960. "Federal-Quapaw Relations, 1800–1833." *Arkansas Historical Quarterly* 19:61–74.   (21)

[103]   Lutz, J. J. 1905–6. "The Methodist
        Missions among the Indian Tribes in
        Kansas." *Transactions of the Kansas State
        Historical Society* 9:160–235.   (33)

[104]   Lyons, Emory J. 1945. *Isaac McCoy: His
        Plan of and Work for Indian Colonization.*
        Fort Hays Kansas State College Studies,
        History Series, no. 1. Topeka: Kansas
        State Printing Plant.   (13)

[105]   McCluggage, Robert W. 1970. "The
        Senate and Indian Land Titles, 1800–
        1825." *Western Historical Quarterly*
        1:415–25.   (9)

[106]   McCoy, Isaac. 1828 [pub. 1936]. "Jour-
        nal of Isaac McCoy for the Exploring
        Expedition of 1828," ed. Lela Barnes.
        Kansas Historical Quarterly 5:227–77.   (11)

[107]   ———. 1830 [pub. 1936]. "Journal of
        Isaac McCoy for the Exploring Expedi-
        tion of 1830," ed. Lela Barnes. *Kansas
        Historical Quarterly* 5:339–77.   (11)

[108]   ———. 1840. *History of Baptist Indian
        Missions: Embracing Remarks on the Former*

and Present Condition of the Aboriginal Tribes; Their Settlement within the Indian Territory, and Their Future Prospects. Washington: William M. Morrison. Reprint with new introduction by Robert F. Berkhofer, Jr., New York: Johnson Reprint Corporation, 1970.   (11)

[109]   McCoy, John C. 1886–88. "Survey of Kansas Indian Lands." *Transactions of the Kansas State Historical Society* 4:298–311.   (12)

[110]   McDonald, Daniel. 1899. *Removal of the Pottawattomie Indians from Northern Indiana.* Plymouth, Ind: D. McDonald.   (20)

[111]   Malin, James C. 1921. *Indian Policy and Westward Expansion.* Bulletin of the University of Kansas Humanistic Studies, vol. 2, no. 3. Lawrence: University of Kansas.   (7)

[112]   ———. 1953. *The Nebraska Question, 1852–1854.* Lawrence, Kans.: Published by the author.   (26)

[113]*   Manypenny, George W. 1880. *Our Indian Wards.* Cincinnati: Robert Clarke

and Company. Republished with a new foreword and documentary appendix, New York: Da Capo Press, 1972. (27)

[114] Marberry, M. M. 1847. *The Golden Voice: A Biography of Isaac Kalloch.* New York: Farrar, Straus. (34)

[115] Martin, Calvin. 1976. "Wildlife Diseases as a Factor in the Depopulation of the North American Indian." *Western Historical Quarterly* 7:47–62. (38)

[116] ———. 1978. *Keepers of the Game: Indian-Animal Relationships and the Fur Trade.* Berkeley: University of California Press. (5)

[117] Mathews, John Joseph. 1961. *The Osages: Children of the Middle Waters.* Norman: University of Oklahoma Press. (23,37)

[118] Mayhall, Mildred P. 1962. *The Kiowas.* Norman: University of Oklahoma Press. (23)

[119] Merwin, Ray E. 1905–6. "The Wyandot Indians." *Transactions of the Kansas State Historical Society* 9:73–88. (21)

[120]   Metcalf, P. Richard. 1974. "Who Should
         Rule at Home? Native American Politics
         and Indian-White Relations." *Journal of
         American History* 61:651–65.   (29)

[121]   Meyer, Roy W. 1962. "The Iowa In-
         dians, 1836–1885." *Kansas Historical
         Quarterly* 28:273–300.   (21)

[122]   Miles, William. 1972. "'Enamoured with
         Colonization': Isaac McCoy's Plan of
         Indian Reform." *Kansas Historical Quar-
         terly* 38:268–86.   (19)

[123]   Miner, H. Craig. 1969. "Border Fron-
         tier: The Missouri River, Fort Scott &
         Gulf Railroad in the Cherokee Neutral
         Lands, 1868–1870." *Kansas Historical
         Quarterly* 35:105–29.   (28)

[124]   ———. 1976. *The Corporation and the In-
         dian: Tribal Sovereignty and Industrial
         Civilization in Indian Territory, 1865–
         1907.* Columbia: University of Missouri
         Press.   (28, 42)

[125]* Miner, H. Craig, and William E. Unrau. 1978. *The End of Indian Kansas: A Study of Cultural Revolution, 1854–1871.* Lawrence: Regents Press of Kansas. (26, 37, 42)

[126] Moore, Bessie Ellen. 1939. "Life and Work of Robert Simerwell." M.A. thesis, University of Kansas. (34, 39)

[127] Morrison, T. F. 1935. "Mission Neosho: The First Kansas Mission." *Kansas Historical Quarterly* 4:227–34. (34)

[128] Murphy, Joseph Francis. 1961. "Potawatomi Indians of the West: Origins of the Citizens Band." Ph.D. diss., University of Oklahoma. (29)

[129] Nasatir, Abraham P., ed. 1952. *Before Lewis and Clark: Documents Illustrating the History of the Missouri, 1785–1804.* 2 vols. Saint Louis: Saint Louis Historical Documents Foundation. (15)

[130] Nichols, Alice. 1954. *Bleeding Kansas.* New York: Oxford University Press. (25)

[131]   Nichols, Roy F. 1956. "The Kansas-Nebraska Act: A Century of Historiography." *Mississippi Valley Historical Review* 43:187–212.   (27)

[132]   Nicholson, William. 1934. "A Tour of Indian Agencies in Kansas and the Indian Territory in 1870." *Kansas Historical Quarterly* 3:289–326.   (36)

[133]   Nielson, George R. 1975. *The Kickapoo People*. Phoenix: Indian Tribal Series.   (31)

[134]   Oliphant, J. Orin, ed. 1947. "The Report of the Wyandot Exploring Delegation, 1831." *Kansas Historical Quarterly* 15:248–62.   (17, 30)

[135]   Prucha, Francis Paul. 1962. *American Indian Policy in the Formative Years: The Indian Trade and Intercourse Acts, 1790–1834*. Cambridge: Harvard University Press.   (9)

[136]   ———. 1962. "Thomas L. McKenney and the New York Indian Board." *Mississippi Valley Historical Review* 48:635–55.   (10)

[137] ———. 1963. "Indian Removal and the Great American Desert." *Indiana Magazine of History* 59:299–322. (16)

[138] ———. 1969. "Andrew Jackson's Indian Policy: A Reassessment." *Journal of American History* 56:527–39. (14)

[139]* ———. 1971. "American Indian Policy in the 1840s: Visions of Reform." In *The Frontier Challenge: Responses to the Trans-Mississippi West,* ed. John G. Clark, pp. 81–110. Lawrence: University Press of Kansas. (10)

[140] ———. 1971. "The Image of the Indian in Pre–Civil War America." In *Indiana Historical Society Lectures 1970–1971: American Indian Policy,* pp. 3–19. Indianapolis: Indiana Historical Society. (8)

[141] ———. 1977. *United States Indian Policy: A Critical Bibliography.* Newberry Library Center for the History of the American Indian Bibliographical Series. Bloomington: Indiana University Press. (15)

[142]   *Report with Respect to the House Resolution Authorizing the Committee on Interior and Insular Affairs to Conduct an Investigation of the Bureau of Indian Affairs.* 1953. Washington, D.C.: Government Printing Office. *House Report* no. 2503, 82d Congress, 2d sess., serial 11582.   (3)

[143]*   Richmond, Robert W. 1974. *Kansas: A Land of Contrasts.* Saint Charles, Mo.: Forum Press.   (26)

[144]   Rivers, Theodore John. 1976. "A Study of the Laws of the Ottawa Indians as Preserved in the OTTAWA FIRST BOOK (1850)." *Kansas Historical Quarterly* 42:225–36.   (23)

[145]   Roark, Harry M. 1970. *Charles Journeycake: Indian Statesman and Christian Leader.* Dallas: Taylor Publishing Company.   (30)

[146]   Robinson, Charles. 1898. *The Kansas Conflict.* Lawrence: Journal Publishing Company.   (25)

[147] Rogin, Michael Paul. 1975. *Fathers and Children: Andrew Jackson and the Subjugation of the American Indian.* New York: Alfred A. Knopf. (13)

[148] Rohrbough, Malcolm. 1968. *The Land Office Business: The Settlement and Administration of American Public Lands, 1789–1837.* New York: Oxford University Press. (9)

[149] Romig, Rev. Joseph. 1909–10. "The Chippewa and Munsee (or Christian) Indians of Franklin County, Kansas." *Collections of the Kansas State Historical Society* 11:314–23. (35)

[150] Ross, Edith Connelley. 1928. "The Old Shawnee Mission." *Collections of the Kansas State Historical Society* 17:417–35. (33)

[151] Royce, Charles C., comp. *Indian Land Cessions in the United States.* In *Eighteenth Annual Report of the Bureau of American Ethnology,* pp. 521–997. Washington, D.C.: Government Printing Office. Reprinted, N.Y.: Arno, 1971; N.Y.: AMS, 1973. (viii)

[152]   Rydjord, John. 1968. *Indian Place-Names: Their Origin, Evolution, and Meanings, Collected in Kansas from the Siouan, Algonquian, Shoshonean, Caddoan, Iroquoian, and Other Tongues.* Norman: University of Oklahoma Press.   (15)

[153]*   Satz, Ronald N. 1975. *American Indian Policy in the Jacksonian Era.* Lincoln: University of Nebraska Press.   (14)

[154]   Schoolcraft, Henry R. 1851–57. *Historical and Statistical Information Respecting the History, Conditions and Prospects of the Indian Tribes of the United States.* 6 vols. Philadelphia: Lippincott, Grambo. Index comp. by Francis S. Nichols. Washington: G.P.O., 1954. Reprinted 7 vols., including index. N.Y.: AMS, 1969.   (21, 36)

[155]*   Schultz, George A. 1972. *An Indian Canaan: Isaac McCoy and the Vision of an Indian State.* Norman: University of Oklahoma Press.   (12, 19, 34)

[156]   Sheehan, Bernard W. 1973. *Seeds of Extinction: Jeffersonian Philanthrophy and the*

American Indian. Chapel Hill: University of North Carolina Press. Reprinted, New York: W. W. Norton, 1974. (ix, 7)

[157] Smith, Dwight L., ed. 1949. "The Attempted Potawatomi Emigration of 1839." *Indiana Magazine of History* 45:51–80. (20)

[158] Socolofsky, Homer E. 1956. "How We Took the Land." In *Kansas: The First Century,* ed. John D. Bright, 1:281–306. New York: Lewis Historical Publishing Company. (26)

[159] ———. 1970. "Wyandot Floats." *Kansas Historical Quarterly* 36:241–304. (27)

[160] Spalding, Charles C. 1858. *Annals of the City of Kansas: Embracing Full Details of the Trade and Commerce of the Great Western Plains.* Kansas City: Van Horn and Abeel's Printing House. (22)

[161] Spencer, Rev. Joab. 1907–8. "The Shawnee Indians: Their Customs, Traditions and Folk-lore." *Transactions of the*

Kansas State Historical Society
10:382–401.   (33)

[162]   Stearn, E. Wagner, and Allen E. Stearn.
1945. *The Effect of Smallpox on the Destiny
of the Amerindian.* Boston: Bruce Hum-
phries.   (39)

[163]   Sutton, Imre. 1975. *Indian Land Tenure:
Bibliographical Essays and a Guide to the
Literature.* New York: Clearwater Pub-
lishing Company.   (27)

[164]   Trenholm, Virginia Cole. 1970. *The
Arapahoes, Our People.* Norman: Univer-
sity of Oklahoma Press.   (23)

[165]   Trennert, Robert A., Jr. 1975. *Alternative to Extinction: Federal Indian Policy and
the Beginnings of the Reservation System,
1846–1851.* Philadelphia: Temple Uni-
versity Press.   (24)

[166]   Unrau, William E. 1968. "The Council
Grove Merchants and Kansa Indians."
Kansas Historical Quarterly 34:266–81.   (24)

[167]   ———. 1971. *The Kansa Indians: A History of the Wind People, 1673 —1873.* Norman: University of Oklahoma Press.   (23, 37)

[168]   ———. 1971. "United States 'Diplomacy' with the Dhegiha-Siouan Kansa, 1815–1825." *Kansas Quarterly* 3:39–46.   (17)

[169]   ———. 1973. "The Depopulation of the Dheghia-Siouan Kansa prior to Removal." *New Mexico Historical Review* 48:313–28.   (39)

[170]   ———. 1975. *The Kaw People.* Phoenix: Indian Tribal Series.   (31)

[171]   ———. 1976. "The Mixed-Blood Connection: Charles Curtis and Kaw Detribalization." In *Kansas and the West: Bicentennial Essays in Honor of Nyle H. Miller,* ed. Forest R. Blackburn, pp. 151–61. Topeka: Kansas State Historical Society.   (30)

[172]   ———. 1976. "Removal, Death, and Legal Reincarnation of the Kaw People." *Indian Historian* 9:2–9.   (30)

[173]   Van Every, Dale. 1966. *Disinherited: The Lost Birthright of the American Indian.* New York: William Morrow.   (8)

[174]   Viola, Herman J. 1974. *Thomas L. McKenney: Architect of America's Early Indian Policy, 1816–1830.* Chicago: Swallow Press.   (11)

[175]   Wallace, Ernest, and E. Adamson Hoebel. 1952. *The Comanches: Lords of the Southern Plains.* Norman: University of Oklahoma Press.   (23)

[176]   Washburn, Wilcomb E. 1965. "Indian Removal Policy: Administrative, Historical and Moral Criteria for Judging Its Success or Failure." *Ethnohistory* 12:274–78.   (14)

[177]   ———. 1968. "Philanthropy and the American Indian: The Need for a Model." *Ethnohistory* 15:43–56.   (14)

[178]*   ———. 1975. *The Indian in America.* New York: Harper and Row.   (x)

[179]   Wedel, Waldo R. 1946. "The Kansa In-
         dians." *Transactions of the Kansas Academy
         of Science* 49:1–35.   (38)

[180]   Weslager, C. A. 1972. *The Delaware In-
         dians: A History.* New Brunswick: Rut-
         gers University Press.   (37)

[181]   ———. 1974. "Enrollment List of Chip-
         pewa and Delaware-Munsies Living in
         Franklin County, Kansas, May 31,
         1900." *Kansas Historical Quarterly*
         40:234–40.   (30)

[182]   ———. 1978. *The Delaware Indian West-
         ward Migration, with the Texts of Two
         Manuscripts (1821–22) Responding to
         General Lewis Cass's Inquiries about Lenape
         Culture and Language.* Wallingford:
         Middle Atlantic Press.   (21)

[183]*   Wissler, Clark. 1940. *Indians of the
         United States: Four Centuries of Their His-
         tory and Culture.* N.Y.: Doubleday, Doran
         and Co. Revised edition prepared by
         Lucy Wales Kluckhohn. Garden City,
         N.Y.: Doubleday, 1966.   (ix)

[184]   "Wyandot and Shawnee Lands in Wyandotte County, Kansas." 1919–1922. *Collections of the Kansas State Historical Society* 15:103–80.   (26)

[185]   Young, Mary E. 1955. "The Creek Frauds: A Study in Conscience and Corruption." *Mississippi Valley Historical Review* 42:411–37.   (9)

[186]   ———. 1958. "Indian Removal and Land Allotment: The Civilized Tribes and Jacksonian Justice." *American Historical Review* 64:31–45.   (9)

[187]*   Zornow, William Frank. 1957. *Kansas: A History of the Jayhawk State*. Norman: University of Oklahoma Press.   (26)

Reserves for the Emigrant Indians of Kansas, January 1854
(Final areas before start of major reduction in 1854)

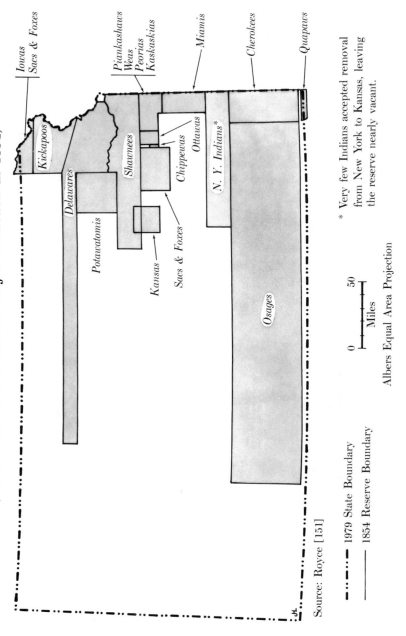

Iowas
Sacs & Foxes
Kickapoos
Delawares
Potawatomis
Kansas
Sacs & Foxes
Shawnees
Piankashaws
Weas
Peorias
Kaskaskias
Chippewas
Ottawas
Miamis
N. Y. Indians*
Cherokees
Osages
Quapaws

* Very few Indians accepted removal
from New York to Kansas, leaving
the reserve nearly vacant.

0   50
Miles

Albers Equal Area Projection

- · - · - 1979 State Boundary
———— 1854 Reserve Boundary

Source: Royce [151]

Reserves for the Emigrant Indians of Kansas, July 1854
(After treaties of 1854 and Kansas—Nebraska Act)

Iowas
Sacs & Foxes
Delawares
Shawnees
Piankashaws
Weas
Peorias
Miamis
Cherokees
Quapaws

Ottawas
Chippewas
N. Y. Indians*

Kickapoos
Potawatomis
Kansas
Sacs & Foxes

Osages

* Very few Indians accepted removal
  from New York to Kansas, leaving
  the reserve nearly vacant.

0   50
Miles

Albers Equal Area Projection

Source: Royce [151]

▪ ▪ ▪ ▪ ▪ 1979 State Boundary
——— 1854 Reserve Boundary

The Newberry Library
Center for the History of the American Indian
Founding Director: D'Arcy McNickle
Director: Francis Jennings

Established in 1972 by the Newberry Library, in conjunction with the Committee on Institutional Cooperation of eleven midwestern universities, the Center makes the resources of one of America's foremost research libraries in the Humanities available to those interested in improving the quality and effectiveness of teaching American Indian history. The Newberry's collections include some 100,000 volumes on the history of the American Indian and offer specialized resources for studying historical aspects of Indian-White relations and Indian linguistics. The Center also assists Native Americans engaged in writing tribal histories and developing educational materials.

ADVISORY COMMITTEE

Chairman: Alfonso Ortiz
University of New Mexico

Robert F. Berkhofer
University of Michigan

Robert V. Dumont, Jr.
Native American Educational Services/Antioch College;
Fort Peck Reservation

Raymond D. Fogelson
University of Chicago

·
William T. Hagan
State University of New York College, Fredonia

Nancy O. Lurie
Milwaukee Public Museum

Cheryl Metoyer-Duran
University of California, Los Angeles

N. Scott Momaday
Stanford University

Father Peter J. Powell
St. Augustine Indian Center

Father Paul Prucha, s.j.
Marquette University

Faith Smith
Native American Educational Services/Antioch College;
Chicago

Sol Tax
University of Chicago

Robert K. Thomas
Wayne State University

Robert M. Utley
Advisory Council on Historical Preservation; Washington, D.C.

Antoinette McNickle Vogel
Gaithersburg, MD.

Dave Warren
Institute of American Indian Arts

Wilcomb E. Washburn
Smithsonian Institution